12 WAYS TO USE Vegetables

Artichokes to Zucchini—Dozens of Tasty Tips for Every Last Bite

ISBN 978-0-9858939-3-4

CONTENTS

INTRODUCTION

What can you do with a few carrots? A head of cabbage? A sweet potato?

This "12 Ways" book has been created to inspire you to experiment in the kitchen, and in the process discover that vegetables are tasty and versatile foods, easy to use in at least a dozen different ways. It's meant to push you beyond your comfort zone and encourage you to try all sorts of new ideas for enjoying vegetables in home-cooked breakfasts, lunches, dinners, and snacks.

Try to include at least one or two servings of nutrient-rich vegetables at meals throughout the day. They're easily available, economical, and delicious, plus they provide a rich supply of vitamins, minerals, phytochemicals, and even protein. (See the "Quick Facts" nutritional information provided for each vegetable, uncooked.) Get in the habit of eating a variety of vegetables and paint your plate with all the colors of the rainbow — green, yellow, orange, red, purple, blue, even white and black — for maximum nutritional diversity.

Vegetables are the foundation of traditional diets around the world, including the Mediterranean Diet, Latin American Diet, African Heritage Diet, Asian Diet, and Plant-Based Diet — all of which Oldways promotes. Visit our website (oldwayspt.org) to find hundreds of easy recipes using real foods and to learn how an overall healthy traditional diet featuring vegetables, along with other plant foods such as pulses and whole grains, can help you reap scientifically proven benefits including improved health, lower disease risk, weight loss, and longevity.

As you learn to expand your cooking repertoire with the ideas on these pages, you will also discover new ways to use up what you have on hand, and help in your own way to reduce household food waste, save money, and feed yourself, your family, and your friends.

So grab that squash and get cooking!

Drink Water

Options For Vegetarians:
Eggs and/or Dairy
including Yogurt,
Cheese, Cottage Cheese

Herbs, Spices, Plant Oils

Nuts, Peanuts, Seeds,
Peanut/Nut Butters

Beans, Peas, Lentils, Soy

Whole Grains including Rice,
Barley, Millet, Oats, Quinoa,
Bread, Cereal, Pasta

*Eat these
foods
every
day*

Fruits and Vegetables

Be physically
active.
Cook and
share meals
with family
and friends.

Illustration by George Middleton   © 2013 Oldways Preservation and Exchange Trust   www.oldwayspt.org

The **Oldways Vegetarian & Vegan Diet Pyramid** is your tool to planning a wholesome plant-based eating style from the bottom (most important!) to the top. It's particularly important for vegetarians and vegans to plan their diets well in order to meet all of their nutritional needs for optimal health.

The **Oldways Vegetarian & Vegan Diet Servings Guide** (shown on the next page) can help balance your vegetarian or vegan diet. Choose fewer servings if you are older or less active, and more servings if you are younger and more active. To ensure that you enjoy the benefits of a nutrient-rich diet it's extremely important to eat a wide variety of plant foods – whole grains, legumes, beans, fruits, vegetables, nuts, and seeds. You may want to consult with a registered dietitian to help individualize an eating plan that meets your particular needs.

In addition, it's especially important for vegetarians and vegans to ensure that they get good sources of the following nutrients:

- **Calcium:** Eat two to three servings of calcium-rich foods every day. These include milk, cottage cheese, yogurt, and cheese, and/or calcium-rich tofu, or plant-based milk (soy, almond), kale, broccoli, dried beans, and almonds.

- **Vitamin D:** Get adequate vitamin D through exposure to the sun (about 15 to 30 minutes per day), vitamin-D fortified foods (i.e., milk for vegetarians and soymilk for vegans), and/or a vitamin D supplement (discuss with your physician).

- **Vitamin B12:** This essential nutrient is primarily available through animal foods. Vegetarians may get it in eggs and dairy products; it's recommended that vegans take a B12 supplement daily and vegetarians a few times per week.

OLDWAYS VEGETARIAN & VEGAN DIET SERVINGS GUIDE

Foods	What counts as a serving?	Number of daily servings
Fruits	½ cup fresh, canned, or frozen fruit ¼ cup dried fruit	3–4
Vegetables	½ cup cooked or 1 cup raw vegetables	4–6
Whole Grains	1 slice whole grain bread 1 cup whole grain cereal ½ cup cooked brown rice, pasta, or other whole grains	5–8
Beans, Peas, Lentils, Soy	½ cup cooked beans, peas, or lentils ½ cup tofu 1 cup soy milk	3–6
Nuts, Peanuts, Seeds, Peanut/Nut Butters	Approx. ¼ cup nuts or seeds 2 tablespoons peanut or nut butter	1–3
Herbs, Spices, Plant Oils	Fresh or dried herbs and spices 1 teaspoon extra-virgin olive oil, canola oil, or other plant oil	Herbs/Spices: Use liberally Plant Oils: up to 5
Eggs and/or Dairy	1 egg 1 cup milk or yogurt ¼ cup cheese ½ cup cottage cheese	Eggs: 4–6 per week Dairy: 1–3

Source: Oldways Vegetarian Network Scientific Advisory Committee

12 WAYS TO USE Artichokes

They may look mysterious, but artichokes are a family friendly vegetable. When cooked whole, they're lots of fun to eat! The petals offer up sweet, succulent bites as you pull the bases of them through your teeth, and the heart is a delicious prize. Artichokes also provide vitamins C, K, and B6, as well as fiber, magnesium, and potassium. They are a member of the sunflower family, and if you compare the two, you will see their similarities.

QUICK FACTS

1 medium artichoke

Calories:	64
Fat:	0.41g
Sodium:	120mg
Carbs:	14g
Fiber:	7g
Protein:	3.5g

EASY COOKING

1. **Whole, Boiled:** Rinse the artichokes under cold running water. Cut about an inch straight across off the top and remove most of the stem, making an even cut to help them stand upright. Use kitchen shears to snip the thorns off the petal tips. Spread the petals slightly apart, rub all cut parts with a lemon to help them stay green, and add them to a large pot of salted water. To keep them submerged, place a smaller pot lid on top of them. Bring the water to a boil, reduce the heat, cover, and cook for 30 to 45 minutes, depending on the size. They're done when you can easily pierce the stem end with a sharp knife. Remove from the water with tongs, drain upside down, and serve in bowls with your choice of dipping sauces (herb butter, balsamic vinegar & mustard, tzatziki, etc.).

2. **Whole, Steamed:** Prepare the artichokes as above and place them in a steamer basket, stem side up. Steam for about 40 minutes, until the stems are tender.

3. **Whole, Baked:** Spread pesto between the petals of fresh, prepared artichokes. Double wrap in aluminum foil and bake directly on the oven rack at 400°F for 50 to 60 minutes, until the stems are tender.

4. **Edible Bowls:** Scoop out the middles and fuzzy chokes of cooked artichokes. Fill the "bowl" with bean dip or guacamole, and use the petals as dippers.

5. **Whole, Braised:** Arrange artichokes upright in a slow cooker, sprinkle with garlic, olive oil, and salt. Add a mixture of white wine and water to a depth of 2 inches and cook on high for 3 to 4 hours, depending on their size, until the leaves can be removed easily.

ON THE GRILL

6 Prepare the artichokes as in #1 for boiling, but cut them into halves and remove the fuzzy chokes. Simmer until tender, remove from the water, drain well, and let them cool. Brush with olive oil, sprinkle with salt and pepper, and grill, cut-side down, for about 5 minutes, until lightly charred.

6 WAYS TO USE UP THAT JAR OF ARTICHOKE HEARTS

To save time, look for jars of artichoke hearts marinated in oil, vinegar, and spices. (Buy jars, not cans, for the best flavor and texture.) Once opened, they will last for several months in the refrigerator as long as the contents are well submerged in the marinade. Here are our favorite ways to put them to use:

7 *Mash with cooked potatoes.*

8 *Chop and stir into risotto or whole grain salads.*

9 *Chop and mix into an omelet or quiche.*

10 *Dice and blend into hummus or pesto.*

11 *Add to vegetable sautés and stir-fries.*

12 *Chop and use as a pizza topping.*

12 WAYS TO USE Arugula

QUICK FACTS

1/2 cup arugula

Calories:	3
Fat:	0.1g
Sodium:	3mg
Carbs:	0.4g
Fiber:	0.2g
Protein:	0.3g

A popular Mediterranean green, arugula is beloved for its tangy, peppery flavor. The younger leaves have a milder flavor. Its baby form can be found on its own, washed and ready to eat wherever lettuce mixes are sold. Arugula delivers fiber, vitamins A, C, and K, as well as calcium, plus 3 grams of proteinin a 3.5 ounce serving. Plus, it has long been considered an aphrodisiac and may even help control blood pressure.

BREAKFAST

1. Add a handful of chopped arugula to omelets, scrambled eggs, or tofu scrambles.

DRINKS

2. Combine a bit of baby arugula with kale and spinach to add a little zip to a green smoothie.

APPETIZERS & SNACKS

3. Finely chop arugula and add to the yolk mixture when making deviled eggs.

SALADS

4. **New Twist for a Classic:** Add chopped arugula to potato salad.

5. **Arugula Salad:** Top a bed of baby arugula with any of the following and drizzle with your favorite dressing:

   - Sliced cantaloupe, blueberries, and a few strips of prosciutto
   - Sliced apples, radishes, and shredded red cabbage
   - Sliced beets, oranges, and toasted almond slivers
   - Sliced fennel and strawberries
   - Sliced grapes and apples, toasted walnuts, and crumbled feta

DRESSINGS & SAUCES

6 Substitute arugula for some, or all, of the basil when making pesto.

SANDWICHES, ETC.

7 Use arugula for the greens in paninis.

SOUPS & STEWS

8 Substitute arugula for spinach in vegetable soups.

EASY COOKING

9 **Pasta:** Add several handfuls of roughly chopped arugula to hot cooked pasta along with a bit of olive oil and grated cheese.

10 **Seafood:** Sauté shrimp or scallops in a little olive oil until cooked through. Toss in some halved cherry tomatoes and a handful or two of arugula.

11 **Chicken/Fish:** Serve baked chicken or fish on a bed of arugula.

12 **Pizza:** Top homemade pizza with arugula for the last few minutes of cooking time.

TIME-SAVING TIP

Toss a handful of arugula into stir-fries at the end of cooking.

12 WAYS TO USE Asparagus

A much anticipated spring vegetable, asparagus grown in the United States is generally in season from March through June. Look for robust, bright green spears with tight tips. Cook asparagus as soon as you can, steaming, roasting, stir-frying, or grilling just until tender to capture its crisp texture and haunting, sweet flavor. Pair it with eggs, mushrooms, creamy sauces, pasta, new potatoes, lemon, mustard, tarragon, and balsamic vinegar. If you need to store asparagus for several days, trim the ends of the spears, stand them up in a jar filled with water, and refrigerate.

QUICK FACTS

1 asparagus spear

Calories:	3
Fat:	0g
Sodium:	0g
Carbs:	0.6g
Fiber:	0.3g
Protein:	0.4g

BREAKFAST

1 **Quick Tart:** Cover a lightly baked puff pastry with sautéed asparagus, chopped garlic, and cracked eggs. Bake for 12 minutes and sprinkle with goat cheese as it comes out of the oven. Cut into squares.

2 **Over Easy:** Fry an egg and enjoy over grilled asparagus.

APPETIZERS & SNACKS

3 Combine apple cider vinegar, water, dill, garlic, and salt in a saucepan and bring to a simmer. Fill a jar with raw asparagus spears, as many as will fit standing upright, and pour in the hot liquid. Cover and refrigerate for 8 hours. Drain and serve on a platter with deviled eggs and roasted red peppers.

SALADS

4 Add chopped, grilled asparagus to green salads.

SANDWICHES, ETC.

5 **Swap for Lettuce:** Include shaved raw asparagus in a veggie wrap as a crunchy stand-in for lettuce.

6 **Taco Filling:** Dice raw asparagus and use as a filling for tacos along with goat cheese, cilantro, and hot sauce.

7 **Quick Lunch:** Arrange several tortillas on a baking sheet, cover with cheese, broil for several minutes until the cheese melts, and roll each one around several cooked asparagus spears.

SOUPS & STEWS

8 **Crunchy Topping:** Using a potato peeler, shave asparagus over carrot or tomato soup before serving.

9 **Creamy Soup:** Sauté an onion in a little olive oil in a large saucepan. Add 4 cups vegetable or chicken stock, a bunch of chopped asparagus, and a peeled, diced potato. Simmer for 30 minutes and purée in a food processor. Return to the saucepan, stir in a spoonful of plain Greek yogurt, and season to taste with salt and pepper.

EASY COOKING

10 **Pasta Pairing:** Cut asparagus into small pieces and toss into freshly cooked spaghetti with anything from mushrooms to peas to parsley and sprinkle with Parmigiano Reggiano for a quick vegetable pasta.

11 **Roasted:** Arrange the spears in a greased baking dish, sprinkle with olive oil, salt, and pepper, and roast at 400°F for about 10 minutes. Serve with hummus.

ON THE GRILL

12 Cut thick asparagus spears into 3-inch pieces. Run two small skewers parallel through each piece, creating groups of about 6 pieces per set of skewers, brush with olive oil, sprinkle with salt, and grill for several minutes per side. Add a squeeze of lemon juice before serving.

GIVE IT A TRY

Asparagus spears are often woody at the bottom. Snap off or cut off several inches before preparing. Or, peel each raw spear, which eliminates the need to shorten them and yields tender spears that cook quickly.

12 WAYS TO USE Avocados

Avocados head the list of healthy fruits, although they're usually categorized as a vegetable since they taste so great in salads. Smooth, buttery, and needing nothing but a quick "nick and peel" to eat as a healthy snack, they contain good fats and are linked to reduced risk of chronic diseases. Because they're typically eaten fresh, their important nutrients aren't lost in processing or heating.

QUICK FACTS

1/2 avocado

Calories:	161
Fat:	12g
Sodium:	7mg
Carbs:	9g
Fiber:	7g
Protein:	2g

BREAKFAST

1. Mash half an avocado and spread it on whole grain toast or an English muffin half for a quick breakfast.

DRINKS

2. Add half an avocado to your next smoothie. Experiment with other flavor pairings, such as almond or soy milk, bananas and blueberries, and greens.

APPETIZERS & SNACKS

3. **Party Platter:** Top whole grain crackers or thin slices of toasted baguette with thin slices of avocado and smoked salmon.

4. **Salsa:** Create a deliciously different salsa by combining diced avocado, chopped tomatoes, corn kernels, chopped cilantro, pepper, and cayenne. Serve with tortilla chips.

5. **Green Dip:** Mash a ripe avocado with fresh lemon juice, salt, minced scallions, and diced tomatoes. Serve with carrot and celery sticks.

SALADS

6. **Picnic Favorite:** Toss chopped avocado, boiled new potatoes, diced celery, and diced capers in a mixing bowl. Moisten with a sprinkling of lemon juice and olive oil.

7. **Pasta:** Add diced avocado, diced bell pepper, and sliced scallions to cooled, cooked pasta, and dress with a mixture of olive oil, vinegar, and mustard.

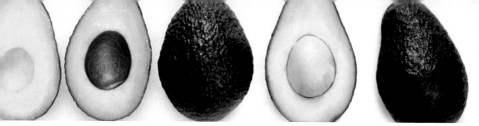

DRESSINGS & SAUCES

8 **For Salads:** In a food processor combine ¼ cup of lemon, lime, or orange juice, 1 small avocado, and a minced garlic clove. With the machine running, add a few tablespoons of olive oil and season to taste with salt and pepper.

9 **For Pasta:** In a food processor combine minced garlic, a few tablespoons of olive oil, 2 chopped avocados, a handful of cherry tomatoes, a sprinkling of Aleppo pepper or hot sauce, and salt and pepper to taste. Blend and use as a sauce for hot cooked, drained pasta. Toss well. (For a shortcut, use guacamole.)

SANDWICHES, ETC.

10 Add sliced avocado to sandwiches, wraps, and tacos. The creamy flavor goes nicely with roasted vegetables, sprouts, greens, and many different kinds of cheese.

SOUPS & STEWS

11 In a blender or food processer, combine several ripe avocados with chicken or vegetable stock, a squeeze of lime juice, and 1 cup plain Greek yogurt to make a creamy soup. Serve chilled.

EASY COOKING

12 Mash a ripe avocado with 1 tablespoon lemon or lime juice, salt, and pepper to make avocado butter; serve on top of a baked potato.

TIME-SAVING TIP

Substitute avocado for another fruit in any sorbet recipe, and include lemon or lime juice to bring out its flavor.

12 WAYS TO USE Beets

You can eat both the red-fleshed root and the green tops of this wonderfully versatile and nutritious vegetable. The earthy, sweet root is a source of folate and manganese, and the tangy greens deliver vitamins A, C, and K. Grocery stores sell fresh beets with their tops, time-saving packaged cooked beets, and canned beets, providing plenty of options for integrating them into your meals any time. Beets are great partners for apples, arugula, avocado, carrots, garlic, anise, caraway and fennel seeds, plain Greek yogurt, goat cheese, mustard, and horseradish.

QUICK FACTS

1 cup diced beets

Calories:	59
Fat:	0.2g
Sodium:	106mg
Carbs:	13g
Fiber:	3.6g
Protein:	2.2g

APPETIZERS & SNACKS

1 **Beet Dip:** Blend roasted beets into your next batch of hummus or bean dip.

SALADS

2 **Spicy & Earthy:** Toss grated, raw beets, or sliced cooked beets, with finely sliced red onion, and dress with red wine vinaigrette and a bit of Dijon mustard. Serve with or without greens.

3 **Picnic Swap:** Replace half the potatoes in your favorite potato salad recipe with golden beets.

4 **Easy Pairing:** Top your favorite salad greens with chopped, roasted beets and goat cheese.

DRESSINGS & SAUCES

5 **Creamy Sauce:** Stir grated, cooked beets, minced garlic, fresh dill or thyme, and salt and pepper into plain Greek yogurt for a colorful sauce to serve with grains or veggie burgers.

SANDWICHES, ETC.

6 **Beyond Mayo:** Stir cooked, grated beets and prepared horseradish into plain Greek yogurt to create a spicy sandwich spread, dip, or sauce for fish or meat.

7 **Lunch Special:** Build a sandwich on your favorite whole grain bread with cream cheese or hummus, baby spinach, and sliced, cooked beets.

EASY COOKING

8 **In the Oven:** Arrange diced beets and other diced root vegetables such as carrots, parsnips, and sweet potatoes on a baking sheet. Sprinkle with chopped fresh rosemary, chopped garlic, and olive oil. Roast at 400°F for about 25 minutes.

9 **Great with Grains:** Stir chopped, roasted beets, crumbled feta, and finely chopped beet greens into cooked farro or brown rice, and drizzle with olive oil and lemon juice.

10 **Braised with Red Cabbage:** Combine sliced beets in a heavy saucepan with sliced red cabbage, sliced beet greens, and diced apple. Sprinkle with apple cider vinegar and caraway seeds, and simmer, covered, for about 30 minutes.

11 **Greens:** Sauté beet greens in olive oil with sliced onions, crushed garlic, salt, and red pepper flakes. Add other greens such as kale or spinach if you wish.

12 **Delicious Dessert:** Poach diced beets in honey (1 part honey: 3 parts beets: 6 parts water) and simmer on low heat until the beets are tender and the liquid is reduced to a syrup. Serve over plain Greek yogurt or vanilla ice cream.

TIME-SAVING TIP

Place whole beets in a microwave-safe dish with a little water in the bottom, cover, and microwave for about 8 minutes.

12 WAYS TO USE Broccoli

QUICK FACTS

1 cup chopped broccoli

Calories:	31
Fat:	0.3g
Sodium:	30mg
Carbs:	6g
Fiber:	2.4g
Protein:	2.6g

Related to cabbage, kale, cauliflower, and Brussels sprouts, broccoli is a vegetable superstar, providing vitamins C and K, iron, and potassium, among other important nutrients. Buy fresh broccoli with firm stalks and tightly closed florets for the best flavor; avoid any with yellow florets, a sure sign that it is past its peak for sweetness. When frozen, broccoli loses its crisp texture, but works well for puréed soup. Broccoli is one of the easiest vegetables to prepare. Chop and cook in boiling salted water for 2 to 3 minutes, or steam for 4 to 6 minutes, being careful not to overcook or lose its bright green color. Serve leftovers with cooked whole grains or in salads, and pair with cheese, chilies, garlic, lemon, miso, soy sauce, pesto, or peanut sauce.

BREAKFAST

1. Add chopped, cooked broccoli to scrambled eggs, omelets, or tofu scrambles.

APPETIZERS & SNACKS

2. Peel the broccoli stalks, cut into thin "trees," add to a platter with other sliced raw vegetables, and serve with your favorite dip.

SALADS

3. **Quick Slaw:** Shred raw broccoli in a food processor, combine with shredded carrots and minced onion, and toss with a bit of red wine vinegar and mustard.

4. **Tabouleh:** Combine cooked bulgur, cooked diced broccoli, diced tomatoes and diced parsley. Toss with olive oil and lemon juice.

5. **Orange & Olive:** Combine cooked, chopped broccoli, chopped olives, and orange segments. Drizzle with olive oil and season with salt and pepper.

SOUPS & STEWS

6. **Hearty Combo:** Sauté an onion in olive oil, then add a peeled, diced potato, chopped broccoli, chopped cauliflower, and vegetable stock to cover. Simmer for about 20 minutes, until the vegetables are tender. Purée and season with salt and pepper.

7 **Tasty Addition:** Add cooked, chopped broccoli to hot vegetable or lentil soup just before serving.

EASY COOKING

8 **Roasted:** Toss chopped broccoli with a little olive oil, arrange on a baking sheet, and roast for 20 minutes at 400°F.

9 **Nutty Pasta:** Combine almond butter, lemon juice, grated fresh ginger, raisins, garlic, salt, and pepper in a food processor to make a smooth sauce. Drizzle over cooked, chopped broccoli and cooked pasta.

10 **Stir-Fry:** Film the surface of a wok or frying pan with olive oil. Heat and stir-fry sliced bell peppers, sliced onions, sliced mushrooms, and chopped broccoli for 3 to 5 minutes, until crisp-tender. Toss with a bit of grated ginger and soy sauce, and serve with brown rice, freekeh, or farro.

11 **Mashed:** Add cooked, chopped broccoli to cooked potatoes, mash, and add olive oil, salt, and pepper.

12 **Topping:** Add lightly cooked, chopped broccoli to pizza just before serving.

GIVE IT A TRY

Peel broccoli stems before chopping and cooking so the stems and florets will cook in the same amount of time.

12 WAYS TO USE Brussels Sprouts

QUICK FACTS

1 cup
Brussels sprouts

Calories:	38
Fat:	0.3g
Sodium:	22mg
Carbs:	8g
Fiber:	3.3g
Protein:	3g

Resembling baby cabbages, Brussels sprouts belong to the Brassica family, and in addition to cabbage, count kale and broccoli as their kin. They offer some fine nutritional benefits and are an excellent source of vitamins C and K. Cook them quickly to enjoy their sweet, nutty flavor. Pair them with apples, carrots, potatoes, capers, caraway seeds, pistachios, maple syrup, or mustard. Remove the cores from larger sprouts with a sharp knife, or the tip of a vegetable peeler, before slicing. Avoid overcooking or boiling, which creates an unpleasant, sulphurous smell. Buy firm, tightly closed heads, free from any yellowing leaves, and refrigerate for up to a week in a loosely sealed plastic bag.

BREAKFAST

1. Add cooked Brussels sprouts to cooked brown rice (or any other whole grain) and top with a poached egg.

SALADS

2. **Shaved:** Remove the cores, quarter, and thinly cut or "shave" Brussels sprouts into thin shreds. Toss with lettuce, diced vegetables of your choice, and your favorite dressing.

3. **Chopped:** Combine shaved Brussels sprouts with diced red peppers, diced fennel, diced carrots, diced cucumbers, and sliced olives, and toss with mustard vinaigrette.

SANDWICHES, ETC.

4. Mix shaved Brussels sprouts with canned tuna and a bit of mayonnaise, and spread on whole grain bread.

SOUPS & STEWS

5. Add a sprinkling of shaved Brussels sprouts to vegetable or creamed soups for a zippy garnish.

EASY COOKING

6 **Mashed:** Combine hot mashed potatoes with cooked Brussels sprouts in a large bowl, and mash to blend, adding a bit of stock and olive oil to obtain the desired consistency. Season with salt and pepper.

7 **Pan-Fried:** Cut Brussels sprouts into quarters and sauté in a single layer in olive oil, stirring frequently over medium-high heat until well browned. Stir in a tablespoon of fig jam mixed with a tablespoon of water and 2 teaspoons of mustard.

8 **Roasted:** Toss Brussels sprouts, cut into halves or quarters, with olive oil and salt. Roast at 400°F for about 15 minutes, until lightly browned.

9 **Sautéed:** Core and slice Brussels sprouts and separate the leaves. Sauté in olive oil until just barely wilted, sprinkle with cumin and salt, and garnish with a small handful of chopped pistachios.

10 **Steamed:** Core and quarter Brussels sprouts, steam for about 4 minutes, and toss with olive oil and lemon juice.

11 **Tacos:** Substitute lightly steamed or shaved Brussels sprouts leaves for lettuce in fish or vegetable tacos.

ON THE GRILL

12 Cook flatbread over medium-high heat for about 1 minute, flip, cover with grated cheese, caramelized onions, and chopped, cooked Brussels sprouts. Cook for 1 minute longer.

TIME-SAVING TIP

Chop leftover cooked Brussels sprouts and add them to stir-fries just a minute or two before serving.

12 WAYS TO USE Cabbage

Different varieties of cabbage all offer inspiration for a number of easy ways to incorporate this humble, healthy ingredient into family meals. Bok choy, green, napa (or Chinese), red, and savoy (or curly) cabbage are excellent sources of vitamins C and K. Look for tight heads of cabbage and discard any loose or browned leaves. Raw or lightly cooked cabbage has a delicious, sweet, mild flavor and adds a welcome crunch to salads and sandwiches. It's a perfect partner for apples, fennel, carrots, celery and caraway seeds, lemon juice, and apple cider, balsamic, and sherry vinegars.

QUICK FACTS

1 cup chopped cabbage

Calories:	22
Fat:	0.1g
Sodium:	16mg
Carbs:	5g
Fiber:	2.2g
Protein:	1.1g

APPETIZERS & SNACKS

1. Use the white ends of napa cabbage, cut into wide strips, to scoop up dips such as hummus or baba ghanoush.

SALADS

2. **Nutty Slaw:** Cut napa cabbage into thin shreds and toss with a simple vinaigrette (1 part vinegar or lemon juice: 2 parts olive oil; plus fresh herbs, mustard, honey, and/or spices). Top with a handful of chopped nuts or sunflower seeds.

3. **Picnic Favorite:** Slice red and green cabbage, sprinkle with a few tablespoons of vinegar and a little sugar, and let sit for a few minutes.

4. **Celery Substitute:** Substitute finely chopped napa or green cabbage for the celery in Waldorf salad, chicken or tuna salad, or whole grain salads.

5. **Beet & Orange:** Combine shredded red cabbage with julienned beets and a pinch of orange zest. Dress with vinaigrette.

SANDWICHES, ETC.

6. Shred napa or savoy cabbage and use in place of lettuce in sandwiches, wraps, and tacos.

SOUPS & STEWS

7 **Final Touch:** Coarsely chop bok choy and drop it into simmering chicken soup or broth a few minutes before serving.

8 **Thickener:** Add finely chopped cabbage to vegetable soup and simmer for about 15 minutes to thicken the broth.

EASY COOKING

9 **Simple Sauté:** Roughly chop and sauté baby bok choy and chopped broccolini with garlic and olive oil.

10 **Side Dish:** Braise thinly sliced red cabbage with onions, apples, and apple cider vinegar. Add a few fennel or caraway seeds.

11 **Roll-Ups:** Simmer large savoy or green cabbage leaves until soft, about 5 minutes, and then fill with seasoned rice, quinoa, or whole wheat couscous. Roll up tightly and tie with kitchen twine. Simmer the rolls in tomato sauce or broth until the cabbage is tender and the rolls are heated through. Remove the twine and serve hot.

ON THE GRILL

12 Cut a head of red or green cabbage in half through the core, lay the cut sides down and slice into 2-inch pieces. Brush both sides with olive oil and sprinkle with salt. Grill on a well-oiled grate or grill pan until charred.

TIME-SAVING TIP

Slice cabbage ahead of time. It will keep for at least 5 days in the refrigerator in a perforated plastic bag.

1 medium carrot	
Calories:	25
Fat:	0.1g
Sodium:	42mg
Carbs:	6g
Fiber:	1.7g
Protein:	0.6g

Carrots are widely available in a rainbow of colors — different shades of orange plus yellow, white, red, and purple. They provide beta-carotene, most accessible when they're cooked or juiced, and are a source of vitamins A, B6, and C, among many other nutrients. Carrots lend themselves to many different cooking methods, including steaming, roasting, sautéing, braising, and enjoying raw. Pair them with beets, fennel, peas, potatoes, almonds, dried cherries and cranberries, raisins, orange, pineapple, maple syrup, and ginger. Carrots keep well in the refrigerator, making them a reliable fresh household staple.

BREAKFAST

1. **Salmon Substitute:** Spread hummus or cream cheese on a bagel or piece of toast and top with thinly sliced raw or roasted carrots, and a bit of onion.

DRINKS

2. Juice carrots, raw peeled ginger, and an apple.

APPETIZERS & SNACKS

3. Toast several slices of French bread, brush with olive oil, and top with fresh ricotta, roasted carrot slices, and a sprinkle of fresh, minced rosemary.

SALADS

4. **New Twist:** Use a vegetable peeler to shave long, thin carrot curls and toss with sesame dressing.

5. **Quick Combo:** Combine diced carrots, peas, edamame, corn, and chopped olives. Toss with your favorite dressing and serve with salad greens.

6. **Tasty Trio:** Add shredded or grated carrots to a green salad along with dried cranberries and chopped pecans. Sprinkle with poppy seed dressing.

DRESSINGS & SAUCES

7 Combine rice vinegar, sweet miso, chopped carrots, and fresh ginger in a blender. Add water to cover and blend until smooth.

SANDWICHES, ETC.

8 **Veggie Special:** Spread a piece of lavash bread with hummus. Add shredded carrots, diced cucumber, lettuce, sprouts, and a bit of cilantro. Roll and enjoy whole, or cut into several pieces.

SOUPS & STEWS

9 Add chopped carrots to just about any slow-cooking dish that includes onions and other veggies.

EASY COOKING

10 **Roasted:** Slice carrots on the diagonal, toss with olive oil, season with salt and pepper, and bake at 400°F for about 15 minutes. Toss with plain Greek yogurt-tahini dressing.

11 **Ginger Braise:** Sauté a minced onion in a large skillet. Add carrots sliced on the diagonal, a bit of maple syrup, minced fresh ginger, and water to cover the bottom of the pan. Bring to a boil, reduce heat to medium-low, and cook until the carrots are tender and the water is almost all cooked away.

ON THE GRILL

12 Place pieces of naan over the fire and heat for about a minute. Flip and add goat cheese, shredded carrots, sesame seeds, and a bit of olive oil. Serve warm.

GIVE IT A TRY

Both flavor and nutritional benefits can be lost when you peel carrots. Instead of peeling, scrub them well and experiment to develop your own guidelines for taste and texture.

12 WAYS TO USE Cauliflower

Cauliflower is an amazingly versatile ingredient that can be enjoyed raw as well as cooked. It joins the plate as a legitimate vegetable, but can also stand in as a substitute for starchy foods like potatoes and rice. Its mild flavor makes cauliflower easy to incorporate into a wide range of dishes while providing fiber, vitamins, and antioxidants. Roast and toss with cooked whole grains for a satisfying meal. Although the white variety is the most well-known, cauliflower can also be orange, green, or purple. Steaming and roasting are popular cooking methods, but keep a close eye on it as it cooks — cauliflower can go from "not quite done" to mushy very quickly.

QUICK FACTS

1 cup chopped cauliflower

Calories:	27
Fat:	0.3g
Sodium:	32mg
Carbs:	5g
Fiber:	2.1g
Protein:	2.1g

APPETIZERS & SNACKS

1. **Marinated:** Cook florets in boiling salted water for about 2 minutes, drain well. Combine vinegar, garlic, mustard seeds, hot pepper, and minced garlic in a saucepan, bring to a boil, and pour over the cauliflower. Cover and chill for 6 to 8 hours.

2. **Healthy Dip:** Blend roasted cauliflower with plain Greek yogurt and season to taste with smoked paprika and garlic powder. Chill for an hour and serve with fresh veggies.

SALADS

3. Toss roasted florets in vinaigrette, add olives, capers, and grape tomatoes, and serve with or without lettuce.

SOUPS & STEWS

4. **Quick Lunch:** Cook florets in chicken or vegetable stock with herbs, onion, celery, garlic, and carrots. Purée for a thick, satisfying soup.

5. **Smart Swap:** Substitute puréed, cooked cauliflower for some or all of the cream in your favorite cream soups to lighten them up and add fiber and other nutrients.

EASY COOKING

6 **Roasted:** Toss cauliflower florets in olive oil, salt, and pepper. Roast at 400°F for 25 to 30 minutes in a single layer on a baking sheet until tender and golden brown.

7 **Stand in for Mashed Potatoes:** Steam florets until tender, then purée them with milk, a drizzle of olive oil, and salt and pepper to taste.

8 **Weeknight Supper:** Add lightly steamed florets to your favorite macaroni and cheese recipe.

9 **Breaded:** Dip slices of cauliflower in an egg wash and dredge in seasoned whole grain panko breadcrumbs. Bake at 400°F for 25 to 30 minutes, or until the cauliflower is cooked through and the coating is crisp.

10 **Aloo Ghobi:** Sauté an onion and some garlic with cumin seeds, turmeric, ginger, and coriander. Add canned tomatoes, roasted chilies, cauliflower florets, and cubes of potato. Simmer for about 20 minutes, until all the vegetables are tender.

11 **"Rice":** Run florets through the food processor until the pieces are about size of grains of rice. Spread out in a thin layer on a baking sheet and bake at 425°F for 7 minutes, toss, and bake for another 7 minutes. Season to taste and serve with stews, curries, or other dishes as a substitute for rice.

12 **Whole:** Remove the outer leaves and trim the stem from a head of cauliflower, being careful to keep the florets attached. Place in a greased pie plate, drizzle with olive oil, sprinkle with salt and pepper, and bake at 400°F for about 50 minutes, until browned and easy to pierce with a skewer. Cut into wedges and serve.

TIME-SAVING TIP

Wrap a head of cauliflower in a clean kitchen towel and bang it on the counter, stem side up, 3 or 4 times, to loosen the florets. Separate them with your hands, and then chop if you want smaller pieces.

12 WAYS TO USE Celery

QUICK FACTS

1 stalk celery

Calories:	6
Fat:	0.1g
Sodium:	32mg
Carbs:	1.2g
Fiber:	0.6g
Protein:	0.3g

With its crispy crunch, celery adds texture and aromatic flavor to a wide range of recipes, but it also deserves to be appreciated as a vegetable that can stand on its own. A low-calorie queen, providing about 6 calories per stalk, celery is 95% water, making it a good hydrating raw snack for hot summer days. It also provides about 30% of our daily requirement for vitamin K, and is linked to benefits for improved digestion. Pale green Pascal celery varieties are most common, but keep your eye out for red celery, which develops a stunning rhubarb color on the lower portions of the stalks. And don't toss away those celery leaves, which resemble giant parsley and can be used in similar ways, added to salads or diced as a garnish.

APPETIZERS & SNACKS

1. **Party Food:** Serve celery stalks with Mediterranean dips such as hummus, baba ghanoush, and tzatziki.

2. **Ants on a Log:** Fill celery stalks with peanut butter, almond butter, or cream cheese and top with raisins.

SALADS

3. **Waldorf:** Toss chopped celery, diced apples, halved grapes, and chopped walnuts with a spoonful of mayonnaise flavored with a bit of Dijon mustard. Add diced or shredded cabbage if you wish.

4. **Avocado & Fennel:** Combine sliced celery with grapefruit sections, sliced avocado, and sliced fennel, and dress with a spoonful of orange juice or your favorite dressing.

5. **Mixed Greens:** Add celery sliced on the diagonal.

SANDWICHES, ETC.

6. Add diced celery to egg, tuna, shrimp, or chicken salad for an extra crunch.

SOUPS & STEWS

7 Sauté celery along with onions and other vegetables when making vegetable soups or chili.

EASY COOKING

8 **Tuna & Beans:** Sauté chopped onion and celery in a little olive oil until soft; add one can drained, canned beans and one can drained, flaked canned tuna. Stir and cook over low heat for several minutes, until hot.

9 **Side Dish:** Steam chopped celery for several minutes, until tender. Sprinkle with salt and chopped fresh herbs.

10 **Braised:** Cut celery stalks into 2- to 3-inch pieces, arrange in a skillet and add vegetable or chicken stock to barely cover the stalks. Bring to a boil, reduce the heat to low, cover, and simmer for about 20 minutes. Serve hot.

ON THE GRILL

11 **Whole:** Lightly oil stalks and grill until tender.

12 **Wrapped:** Cut stalks into 2-inch pieces, arrange on a square of heavy-duty aluminum foil, sprinkle with olive oil and salt, wrap to form a tight packet, and grill for about 10 minutes.

TIME-SAVING TIP

Dice celery along with a small tomato, and use uncooked as an omelet filling or to add texture to scrambled eggs.

12 WAYS TO USE Corn

Sweet corn is one of the most popular vegetables around. It's the perfect partner for beans, tomatoes, peppers, summer squash, onions, avocados, and fresh herbs including basil, cilantro, tarragon, and thyme, and is a great addition to soups, chowders, and whole grain dishes. Plus, corn is a source of protein and fiber, and delivers vitamins B and C. Enjoy corn-on-the-cob in season, as soon as possible after it has been picked. Simply shuck it, place in a large pot with about an inch of water in the bottom, bring to a boil, cover, and cook for about 5 minutes. Keep canned corn and frozen corn on hand for quick weekday meals, and experiment to discover your favorite ways to incorporate it into soups, salads, and other dishes.

QUICK FACTS

1 cup corn	
Calories:	125
Fat:	1.82g
Sodium:	22mg
Carbs:	29.29g
Fiber:	2.9g
Protein:	4.7g

BREAKFAST

1. **With Eggs:** Add corn and diced red pepper to scrambled eggs and frittatas.

2. **Savory Treat:** Mash a cooked sweet potato, top with corn and chopped scallions, and heat in the microwave. Add a dollop of cottage cheese and season with salt and pepper.

APPETIZERS & SNACKS

3. **Salsa:** Combine diced tomatoes, hot peppers, onions, corn, and beans, and season with olive oil, lime juice, salt, and pepper. Serve with tortilla chips.

4. **Enhanced Dip:** Add corn and diced tomatoes to guacamole.

SALADS

5. Add corn to an arugula and farro salad, sprinkle with crumbled goat cheese and chopped scallions, and drizzle with vinaigrette.

SANDWICHES, ETC.

6. **Veggie Burrito:** Wrap up beans, rice, lettuce, tomatoes, chopped onions, corn, salsa, guacamole, and a bit of shredded cheese in a flour or corn tortilla.

SOUPS & STEWS

7 **Weeknight Supper:** Sauté an onion in a little olive oil, add a diced red or green bell pepper (or a diced hot pepper), several diced tomatoes, a can of drained, rinsed black or pinto beans, and 1 to 2 cups of corn. Cook for about 30 minutes and season with salt and pepper. Serve with rice.

EASY COOKING

8 **Quick Hash:** Cook diced onion, diced green pepper, chopped cooked potatoes, and corn in a bit of olive oil in a heavy skillet, turning several times with a spatula until lightly browned.

9 **Creamed Corn:** Combine 2 cups corn with 1 cup milk and a little honey in a saucepan, stir well, and cook over low heat for about 10 minutes. Add a sprinkling of chopped basil or tarragon.

10 **Instant Succotash:** Combine frozen corn with frozen edamame, microwave until heated through, and toss with your favorite dressing.

11 **Weeknight Dinner:** Combine corn, cooked quinoa (or any other whole grain), tomatoes, chopped roasted chilies, and red kidney beans. Season with salt and pepper.

ON THE GRILL

12 Cook corn-on-the-cob over a medium-high fire for about 4 minutes, turning several times to create grill marks. Spread with plain Greek yogurt and season with smoked salt and pepper.

GIVE IT A TRY

Add leftover cooked corn to baked beans.

12 WAYS TO USE Cucumbers

One of summer's favorite foods, cucumbers are prized for their thirst-quenching juice and pleasant crunch. They're delicious additions to green salads, fruit salads, snack plates, sandwiches, and other dishes that benefit from a bit of texture. In addition to the common garden varieties, you can find Armenian cucumbers, known for their delicate flavor and edible peel. Small pickling cucumbers contain less water than others, but can also be enjoyed raw. Cucumbers lose moisture quickly once they're harvested, causing them to become soft. Don't buy more than you can use in a day or two, and store them in an unsealed plastic bag in the refrigerator. Peeling is optional, or you can rake them with a fork and then slice, so bits of skin show at the edges.

QUICK FACTS

1 medium cucumber

Calories:	24
Fat:	0.32g
Sodium:	4mg
Carbs:	4.3g
Fiber:	1.4g
Protein:	1.19g

BREAKFAST

1. Add sliced cucumbers and lox to pumpernickel toast and top with finely sliced red onions and capers.

DRINKS

2. Blend cucumber, spinach, apple, ginger, mint, and lemon and serve over ice for a refreshing summer cooler.

APPETIZERS & SNACKS

3. Substitute thick cucumber slices for bread and top with egg salad, baba ghanoush, or rounds of goat cheese.

SALADS

4. **Mediterranean Classic:** Mix together chopped cucumber, chopped tomatoes, olives, and feta cheese. Drizzle with balsamic dressing.

5. **Boats:** Cut a cucumber in half, scoop out the seedy part, and fill with chicken or tuna salad.

6. **Grape-Yogurt:** Cut cucumbers into thin slices, place in a colander, sprinkle with salt, and let sit for about 30 minutes. Pat dry with paper towels and toss with sliced grapes, plain Greek yogurt, and a sprinkling of chopped, fresh dill.

7 **Asian:** Toss sliced cucumbers with a spoonful of tamari.

8 **Summer Favorite:** Combine chopped cucumbers with chopped zucchini, sprinkle with salt and vinegar, and let sit for 20 minutes. Drain, add chopped tomatoes and corn, and season with salt and pepper. Add a can of drained, rinsed beans if you wish.

SANDWICHES, ETC.

9 Spread whole grain bread with hummus or plain Greek yogurt, top with sliced cucumbers, and cut into triangles.

SOUPS & STEWS

10 Garnish gazpacho and other cold soups with diced cucumber.

EASY COOKING

11 Use a spiralizer to make long, thin, pasta-like cucumber strands. Toss with pesto or tomato sauce, and sprinkle with cheese.

ON THE GRILL

12 Grill naan over a medium-hot fire for about 1 minute. Turn, spread with goat cheese, top with chopped cucumbers, olive oil, salt, and pepper, and cook for about 1 minute longer.

TIME-SAVING TIP

Peel and seed cucumbers, chop, sauté for a few minutes, then season with salt and pepper.

12 WAYS TO USE Eggplant

A Mediterranean Diet staple, eggplant is loaded with vitamins and minerals. It is delicious paired with chickpeas, garlic, bell peppers, celery, onions, summer squash, tomatoes, basil, olives, and capers, served with rice or couscous. It also tastes wonderful in Asian dishes with peanut or teriyaki sauce. In addition to the popular large purple-black variety, you can find white eggplant, purple and white striped eggplant, and long, slender Asian eggplant. At peak ripeness, all varieties are firm and shiny. Store at room temperature and use within a day or two; eggplant doesn't benefit from being chilled.

BREAKFAST

1 Add leftover cooked eggplant or ratatouille to omelets or frittatas.

APPETIZERS & SNACKS

2 **Roll-Ups:** Cut a large unpeeled eggplant lengthwise into ¼-inch-thick slices, arrange on a baking sheet and bake at 400°F for 15 minutes. Top each slice with warm tomato sauce, grated Parmigiano Reggiano, and chopped basil. Roll up and secure with toothpicks.

3 **Tasty Dip:** Bake a whole eggplant on a baking sheet at 350°F until soft, about 45 minutes. Scoop the flesh into a food processor and add plain Greek yogurt, tahini, lemon juice, chopped garlic, and cumin. Blend until smooth, stir in chopped parsley by hand, and serve as a dip with bread or veggies.

4 **Sweet & Sour:** Combine an unpeeled, diced eggplant in a large saucepan with about ¼ cup water, a spoonful of raisins, a bit of sugar, wine vinegar, and the surprise ingredient — a square or two of dark chocolate. Cover and cook over low heat for 25 minutes, stirring frequently. Sprinkle with lemon zest and let cool.

SANDWICHES, ETC.

5 Cook sliced, unpeeled eggplant in a nonstick skillet for about 10 minutes, until very soft. Spread about 1 tablespoon of goat cheese on both halves of a whole wheat sandwich roll or English muffin and bake at 275°F for 8 to 10 minutes. Remove from the oven and top the bottom half with eggplant, sliced tomato, and arugula.

EASY COOKING

(6) **On Pizza:** Bake a whole wheat pizza crust on a baking sheet at 450°F until the bottom is crisp (approximately 3 minutes). Turn the crust over. Add marinara sauce, chopped basil, garlic, thinly shaved Parmigiano Reggiano, and eggplant cubes. Bake 12 to 15 minutes more.

(7) **Quick Dish:** Roast eggplant cubes with sliced zucchini, peppers, and onions on a baking sheet at 400°F for about 20 minutes. Combine with couscous or quinoa, add olives and chickpeas, and splash with lemon juice and olive oil.

(8) **Oven Stew:** Roast eggplant cubes, diced potatoes, and cherry tomatoes at 400°F in a casserole dish for about 25 minutes. Add a few tablespoons of pesto, toss, and serve.

(9) **Pasta Topping:** Peel eggplant and cut into ½-inch cubes. Sauté in olive oil until brown on all sides. Add garlic, crushed or diced tomatoes, and basil. Serve over whole wheat pasta.

(10) **Partner for Tomatoes:** Chop an unpeeled eggplant, toss with olive oil, sprinkle with salt, and roast at 400°F for 10 to 15 minutes along with a box of halved cherry tomatoes.

ON THE GRILL

(11) **Simple Side:** Brush sliced eggplant on both sides with olive oil. Grill until tender, turning once.

(12) **First Course:** Spread each slice of grilled eggplant with 1 teaspoon of pesto and top with a sliced tomato, mozzarella, and basil. Drizzle with olive oil and balsamic vinegar.

GIVE IT A TRY

As eggplant sits after harvesting it can turn bitter. If you buy it at the store, where it may have been chilled, cut it into cubes, sprinkle with salt, let sit in a colander in the sink for 30 minutes. Drain, rinse, and pat dry with paper towels before using.

12 WAYS TO USE Green Beans

QUICK FACTS

1 cup chopped green beans

Calories:	31
Fat:	0.2g
Sodium:	6mg
Carbs:	7g
Fiber:	2.7g
Protein:	1.8g

Fresh green snap beans, plus their yellow and purple cousins, are one of the great treats of summer. (Old-timers called them string beans, before modern varieties were bred to eliminate the tough strings.) For the very sweetest flavor, seek fresh, skinny green beans, no thicker than a chopstick, and all about the same length for uniform cooking. Avoid thicker beans with visible seeds, which will tend to be tough. Snap or cut off the ends (a process called topping and tailing), leave them whole or chop them, and cook quickly in boiling water or steam them just until tender, but still crunchy. Sprinkle lightly with salt or add a bit of olive oil and they're ready to serve.

BREAKFAST

1. Toss cooked, chopped green beans with pesto. Serve on toast, topped with a poached egg.

APPETIZERS & SNACKS

2. **For Dipping:** Include tender, raw, whole green beans along with other veggies and serve with hummus.

3. **Dilly Beans:** Fill sterilized canning jars with a peeled garlic clove and a pinch of dill seeds. Pack with beans standing up lengthwise, cover with a mixture of vinegar, water, and salt brought to a boil, and process jars according to the manufacturer's instructions.

SALADS

4. **Family Favorite:** Combine drained, rinsed kidney and garbanzo beans with slightly cooked chopped green and/or yellow beans, chopped roasted red peppers, and diced scallions. Toss with vinaigrette.

5. **Niçoise:** Top lettuce with sliced, ripe tomatoes, halved hard-boiled eggs, chopped cooked potatoes, tuna, black niçoise olives, and cooked green beans. Drizzle with vinaigrette.

6. **Chopped:** Combine diced, cooked green beans with diced carrots, diced celery, diced tomatoes, and drained, rinsed canned beans. Season with salt and pepper or your favorite dressing.

SOUPS & STEWS

(7) Add chopped beans to minestrone and vegetable soups and stews during the last 30 minutes of cooking time.

EASY COOKING

(8) **Blanched:** Bring a pot of salted water to a boil, add beans, cover and cook for 3 to 5 minutes, until the beans are tender. Toss with olive oil and lemon juice; season with salt and pepper.

(9) **Braised:** Sauté an onion and garlic in olive oil, add red pepper flakes and diced cherry tomatoes, and cook for about 5 minutes. Stir in chopped green beans and a little wine, cover, and simmer for about 15 minutes, until the beans are very tender.

(10) **Steamed:** Steam chopped beans over boiling water for about 5 minutes. Add to hot, sautéed mushrooms and red peppers, and top with mustard vinaigrette.

(11) **Thanksgiving Must-Have:** Combine cooked, chopped green beans with mushroom cream sauce and fried onions, top with additional fried onions, and bake at 350°F for about 25 minutes.

(12) **Weeknight Dinner:** Add cooked, chopped green beans and halved cherry tomatoes to hot pasta. Toss with olive oil, salt, pepper, and Parmigiano Reggiano.

TIME-SAVING TIP

If you're preparing a lot of beans for cooking, line up about 10 at a time and trim them all at once with two knife strokes.

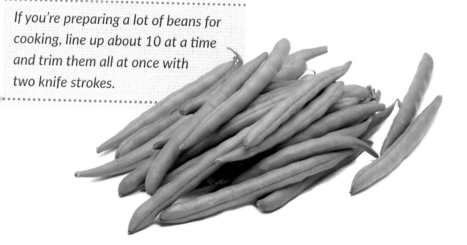

12 WAYS TO USE Greens

Leafy greens such as kale, collards, Swiss chard, and spinach are nutrient powerhouses. For example, you get more than 600% of your daily value of vitamin K, more than 200% of your daily value of vitamin A, and more than 130% of vitamin C in just 1 cup chopped raw kale. Experiment with greens in their baby and full-grown sizes and use them interchangeably to discover the versatility of their unique flavors. Pull off the tough stems, wash the leaves well in several changes of warm water, dry well, and thinly slice or dice to create the perfect addition to a wide range of dishes.

BREAKFAST

1. **Smoothie:** Blend together 2 cups chopped greens, 2 celery stalks, ½ cup berries, 1 tablespoon peanut butter, parsley, and ½ to 1 cup water, soy or almond milk, or coconut water (depending on desired thickness).

2. **With Eggs:** Stir diced raw greens into scrambled eggs, quiches, or frittatas.

APPETIZERS & SNACKS

3. **Oven Crisps:** Toss kale leaves (stems removed) with olive oil, minced garlic, salt and pepper. Spread on a baking sheet and roast in the oven at 375°F for about 20 minutes, stirring every 5 minutes, until leaves are crispy on the edges and tender in the center.

4. **Special Hummus:** Toss kale or spinach leaves into the food processor with a can of chickpeas, a squeeze of lemon, olive oil, and a dollop of tahini.

SALADS

5. Remove the stems from greens, cut into thin slivers, and place in a salad bowl. Drizzle with olive oil and sprinkle with salt. Massage to slightly bruise the cut leaves, making them tender. Add raisins and walnuts.

DRESSINGS & SAUCES

6. Add chopped greens to basil pesto, or use greens exclusively in place of basil or other herbs.

SANDWICHES, ETC.

7 Add baby greens to wraps in place of lettuce.

SOUPS & STEWS

8 Add thinly sliced or minced greens to vegetable soups and stews, especially those with a tomato base.

EASY COOKING

9 **Mashed:** Mash together lightly sautéed greens, cooked potatoes, and warm buttermilk or soy milk, along with a handful of grated cheese.

10 **With Pasta:** Stir sliced raw greens into your next batch of tomato sauce, simmer for about 5 minutes, and serve over whole grain pasta.

11 **Sautéed:** Heat a large, heavy skillet, spray with olive oil, and sauté diced fresh greens for about 5 minutes over medium-high heat, tossing several times, until wilted. Season with salt and pepper, and serve warm.

12 **On Pizza:** Put coarsely chopped greens under the cheese on a pizza for a tender topping, or over the cheese to let them get crispy.

TIME-SAVING TIP

Heat leftover chopped greens in a skillet, add a beaten egg, and cook, tossing, for a minute or two.

12 WAYS TO USE Mirepoix

QUICK FACTS

1/2 cup mirepoix

Calories:	42
Fat:	2.4g
Sodium:	33 mg
Carbs:	5g
Fiber:	1.4g
Protein:	0.7g

Mirepoix (pronounced meer-pwah) is a finely chopped mixture of onion, carrot, and celery, in a ratio of 2 parts onion to 1 part each carrot and celery. Sautéed in butter or olive oil to soften and meld the tastes, this simple mixture adds a depth of flavor to a variety of dishes. Store leftovers in the refrigerator and use within about three days of preparing. In addition to supplying texture and fresh aromas, mirepoix delivers half of your daily vitamin A requirement.

BREAKFAST

1. **With Eggs:** Add mirepoix to eggs before scrambling or making a frittata or quiche.

2. **Veggie Special:** Add mirepoix to a red pepper and tofu scramble.

DRESSINGS & SAUCES

3. **Flavor Boost:** Add mirepoix to gravies and tomato sauces for added texture and taste.

4. **Seafood Partner:** Top off fish dishes with a spoonful or two of mirepoix.

5. **Extra Special:** Add a splash of white wine once mirepoix is sautéed, then add vegetable broth and simmer to make a sauce for whole grains, roasted vegetables, or flaky white fish.

6. **Exotic:** Add finely chopped garlic and ginger to mirepoix, sauté until softened, then add turmeric, cinnamon, and paprika to form the base for lentils and other North African dishes.

SANDWICHES, ETC.

7. Add mirepoix to your favorite veggie burger mixture. Or, use it as a topping.

SOUPS & STEWS

8 **Tasty Stew Base:** After cooking mirepoix in a soup pot, add chopped vegetables of your choice. Cook until softened. Add a sprinkling of dried herbs and cook briefly. Stir in 1 tablespoon of tomato purée, then add beef, chicken, or vegetable stock. Stir again and cook for 20 minutes, or until flavors have mingled. Add beans if you wish.

9 **Added Flavor:** After browning cubed vegetables, remove them from the pot, add mirepoix, and sauté until softened. Continue with your stew recipe.

EASY COOKING

10 **Pasta Pep:** While pasta is cooking, sauté mirepoix, add dried herbs, chopped mushrooms and garlic, and cook for 5 minutes stirring regularly. Add canned tomato sauce and cook for another 5 minutes. Add to drained pasta and serve with grated cheese.

11 **Perk up Grains:** Stir mirepoix into hot, cooked whole grains.

12 **Mac & Cheese:** Add uncooked mirepoix to the milk you use for making mac and cheese. Bring the milk just to a boil, reduce the heat, and simmer for 15 minutes. Strain the milk, discard the mirepoix, and proceed with the recipe.

GIVE IT A TRY

Substitute green and/or red peppers for the carrot in mirepoix to create the Holy Trinity of Cajun and Creole cooking.

12 WAYS TO USE Mushrooms

QUICK FACTS

1 cup sliced mushrooms

Calories:	16
Fat:	0.2g
Sodium:	4mg
Carbs:	2.3g
Fiber:	0.7g
Protein:	2.2g

Mushrooms are treasured for their rich, meaty flavor and detoxifying properties, which link them to reduced risk of heart disease, among other illnesses. Mycophagy — eating mushrooms — dates back to ancient times. More than 20 species are commercially cultivated today, with other varieties foraged by mushroom enthusiasts. A wide variety of mushrooms, including crimini, maitake, oyster, portobello, shitake, and white button are available in most supermarkets. Roasting mushrooms brings out their natural sweetness. Add them to vegetable or whole grain dishes to provide a unique woodsy, buttery flavor and springy texture.

BREAKFAST

1. **Over Easy:** Sauté sliced or chopped mushrooms, top with a beaten egg, and cook until set.

2. **Tasty Pairing:** Add sautéed mushrooms and peppers to omelets, frittatas, or tofu scrambles.

APPETIZERS & SNACKS

3. Roast white button or crimini mushroom caps on a lightly greased baking sheet at 400°F until slightly juicy. Remove from the oven, fill with sautéed bread crumbs, or a dollop of hummus and snipped fresh herbs, and arrange on a serving platter.

SALADS

4. Sauté sliced, lightly salted mushrooms until they start to give off liquid, sprinkle with balsamic vinegar, and serve immediately on top of fresh greens.

DRESSINGS & SAUCES

5. Sauté diced mushrooms in a little olive oil until soft. Sprinkle with flour, cook for about 1 minute, and then add vegetable stock and wine or sherry and salt. Simmer for 10 minutes until thickened. Serve with mashed potatoes.

SANDWICHES, ETC.

6 Slather a whole grain tortilla or flatbread with hummus or baba ghanoush and add a layer of sautéed mushrooms along with roasted peppers and arugula, or your choice of fresh greens.

SOUPS & STEWS

7 **For Contrast:** Add chopped mushrooms to puréed cauliflower or potato soup and cook for about 5 minutes.

8 **Meat Substitute:** Add mushrooms to thick vegetable stew with carrots, potatoes, and celery. Or, chop and add to chili or bean stew.

EASY COOKING

9 **In the Oven:** Toss mushrooms lightly with olive oil and roast on a lightly greased baking sheet at 400°F for about 10 minutes, or until they turn juicy. Toss with your favorite herbs and enjoy as a side or main dish.

10 **Quick Sauté:** Remove the stems, slice the caps, and sauté mushrooms in a little olive oil until soft. Sprinkle in a bit of wine or lemon juice, and some fresh chopped herbs. Enjoy as a side dish, serve as a topping for fish or chicken, or toss with any cooked whole grain.

11 **With Greens:** Sauté sliced mushrooms in a little olive oil along with some chopped onion and garlic, add baby spinach or chopped kale, and sauté for about 4 minutes, until the greens are tender.

ON THE GRILL

12 Remove the stems and brush portobello caps lightly with olive oil. Cook on a lightly oiled grill grate until soft and browned, about 5 minutes. Turn and cook for 5 minutes more. Serve on toasted buns with all the fixings.

TIME-SAVING TIP

Add lightly sautéed mushrooms to your favorite tomato sauce just before serving over pasta.

12 WAYS TO USE Onions

QUICK FACTS

1 cup chopped onion

Calories:	64
Fat:	0.2g
Sodium:	6mg
Carbs:	15g
Fiber:	2.7g
Protein:	1.8g

Onions are members of a large family that includes chives, leeks, scallions, shallots, and garlic. Red, white, and yellow globe-shaped onions are true culinary workhorses that we often reach for automatically as a must-have first ingredient for soups, stews, stir-fries, tomato sauces, and dozens of other dishes. They lend themselves to braising, baking, sautéing, roasting, and grilling, and their sweetest flavors come out when they are caramelized by cooking very slowly over low heat. Pair onions with celery, mushrooms, peppers, tomatoes, zucchini, chickpeas, and thyme. Substitute milder-flavored scallions if you prefer.

BREAKFAST

1. **With Eggs:** Add sautéed chopped onions, peppers, and mushrooms to an omelet, scrambled eggs, or tofu scramble.

2. **Hash:** Combine chopped onions with leftover cooked potatoes and sauté in olive oil, turning occasionally, until lightly browned.

APPETIZERS & SNACKS

3. **Party Toast:** Spread goat cheese on toasted baguette slices and top with caramelized onions.

4. **Guacamole:** Mash an avocado and mix in chopped white onions, chopped tomatoes, chopped cilantro, and lemon juice to taste.

5. **Pickled:** Combine vinegar, sugar, and salt in a saucepan, bring just to a boil, and simmer, stirring until the sugar dissolves. Add sliced red onions, cover, and let sit for 1 hour. Drain. Spread crackers with cream cheese and top with pickled onions.

SALADS

6. Dice a red onion, put it into a strainer, and pour boiling water over it before adding to cole slaw or potato salad, to reduce the bite.

DRESSINGS & SAUCES

7 Add diced sweet onions to vinaigrette and let sit for about 30 minutes before using on a salad.

SANDWICHES, ETC.

8 **Fajitas:** Sauté sliced onions, green and red peppers, and any other vegetables you like. Wrap in a warmed tortilla along with rice and beans, and a dollop of salsa or guacamole.

EASY COOKING

9 **Caramelized:** Fill a slow cooker about ⅔ full with thinly sliced onions, cover, and cook on low for about 10 hours (overnight) until the onions are very soft and brown.

10 **Roasted:** Chop or slice onions, toss with olive oil, season with salt and pepper, and bake at 375°F for about 30 minutes, or until the onions are soft and browned.

ON THE GRILL

11 **Sliced:** Cut onions into thick slices, spray with olive oil, season with salt and pepper, and grill on a well-oiled grate for about 8 minutes, turning once, until soft and lightly browned.

12 **In Foil:** Peel and slice onions and arrange on 12-inch squares of aluminum foil. Drizzle with olive oil, season with salt and pepper, fold up and pinch to make loose packets, and grill for about 30 minutes.

GIVE IT A TRY

Chill onions in the refrigerator for a day or two before cutting and use the sharpest knife you have to reduce tears.

12 WAYS TO USE Peas

QUICK FACTS

1 cup peas

Calories:	118
Fat:	0.6g
Sodium:	7mg
Carbs:	21g
Fiber:	7g
Protein:	8g

Freshly picked peas are a special early summer treat, so sweet and tender they're easy to eat raw, right from the pods. Smart cooks keep a bag or two of frozen peas on hand to enjoy in a number of ways. Above all, avoid overcooking these warm weather gems. Simply put them in a colander, pour boiling water over them, and they're ready to use. Providing protein, vitamins, and fiber, peas make great additions to whole grain and pasta dishes, and pair nicely with carrots, mushrooms, potatoes, onions, and mint. They're also a favorite side dish for salmon. Fresh snap peas make great snacks, fresh snow peas add crunch to stir-fries and salads, and pea tendrils, sometimes available at farmers markets, are delicious when lightly sautéed.

APPETIZERS & SNACKS

1. **On Toast:** Combine lightly cooked fresh, or slightly thawed frozen peas with garlic, chopped mint, olive oil, and salt in a food processor to make a thick purée. Spread on crackers or toasted baguette slices.

2. **With Dips:** Serve snap peas with dips such as hummus, tzatziki, and baba ghanoush.

SALADS

3. **Quick Meal:** Combine cooked Israeli couscous or any cooked whole grain, peas, diced tomatoes, chopped arugula, and sliced olives. Toss with pesto.

4. **Spicy Garnish:** Combine sugar, minced garlic, and vinegar in a saucepan, heat until the sugar dissolves, and pour over frozen peas. Cool and store in the refrigerator for up to a week. Add to tuna or potato salad, or sprinkle on top of green salads.

5. **Fast Lunch::** Combine diced carrots, diced tomatoes, and peas, toss in a vinaigrette, and top with diced parsley or basil.

SOUPS & STEWS

6 **Quick Starter:** Sauté an onion in olive oil, add peas, vegetable stock, tarragon, salt, and pepper, and simmer for 5 minutes. Purée and top with plain Greek yogurt and a sprinkling of diced chives or fresh dill.

7 **Tasty Addition:** Toss some peas into your next batch of vegetable soup or minestrone.

EASY COOKING

8 **Kid Friendly:** Add peas to your favorite mac and cheese recipe just before serving.

9 **Mediterranean Favorite:** Sauté a sliced onion in olive oil in a large skillet, add partially thawed frozen peas and cooked pasta, top with 2 beaten eggs and Parmigiano Reggiano, and toss over medium heat until hot.

10 **Weeknight Supper:** Combine thawed frozen peas and cubed baked tofu with cooked rice, and toss with peanut sauce.

11 **Dash of Color:** Add peas to mashed potatoes or cauliflower.

12 **Quick Side:** Sauté sliced onions and mushrooms until tender, add peas, and cook until heated through.

TIME-SAVING TIP

Add leftover cooked peas to cold pasta salads.

12 WAYS TO USE Peppers (Bell)

QUICK FACTS

1 red bell pepper

Calories:	37
Fat:	0.36g
Sodium:	5mg
Carbs:	7g
Fiber:	2.5g
Protein:	1.18g

Peppers come in all shapes, sizes, and degrees of spiciness, including some that are downright incendiary. Bell peppers are one of the most popular types. They grow in a variety of bright colors in addition to green — red, yellow, purple, whitish-yellow, even red and yellow stripes! — and they provide vitamins A and C, folic acid, and fiber. In fact, red bell peppers pack the most nutrition and are richer in vitamin C than most citrus fruit. Bell peppers add texture along with a touch of sweetness to a wide range of dishes, and are just as delightful raw as they are cooked. Sauté or roast them to bring out their earthy goodness, and partner them with zucchini, tomatoes, mushrooms, onions, potatoes, olives, white beans, and eggs.

BREAKFAST

1. Add diced bell peppers to omelets, quiches, or frittatas.

APPETIZERS & SNACKS

2. **Dippers:** Slice bell peppers into strips and serve with hummus or your favorite dip.

3. **Pickled:** Combine vinegar, water, sugar, salt, and garlic in a saucepan, bring to a boil, add bell pepper strips, and remove from the heat. Cool and store in the refrigerator for up to one week. Serve with olives and other pickled vegetables.

SALADS

4. **Quick Lunch:** Combine canned beans, diced bell peppers, diced celery, onion, lemon or lime juice, a little bit of olive oil, cumin, and cayenne pepper.

5. **Summer Special:** Julienne several bell peppers and a zucchini, toss with a little olive oil, garlic, and vinegar, and marinate for about 4 hours before serving.

DRESSINGS & SAUCES

6. **Salsa:** Combine finely chopped bell peppers with onion, garlic, fresh herbs, red chili flakes, vinegar, and olive oil for a striking sauce to accompany fish.

7 **For Pasta:** Combine roasted bell peppers with Parmigiano Reggiano, garlic, salt, pepper, olive oil, and fresh herbs in a food processor. Use as a pasta sauce.

SANDWICHES, ETC.

8 Add roasted peppers to sandwiches and wraps.

EASY COOKING

9 **Simple Side:** Sauté sliced bell peppers with garlic, sliced onions, and seasoning of your choice in a little olive oil. Add tofu, eggs, or fish for a complete meal.

10 **Boats:** Cut peppers in halves, scoop out the seeds and membranes, stuff with a mixture of cooked rice, onions, tomatoes, and spices. Arrange in a shallow dish and bake at 350°F for 30 minutes.

11 **Weeknight Special:** Sauté sliced onions and sliced peppers, add halved cherry tomatoes, a can of white beans, and chopped fresh baby spinach. Cook for about 10 minutes, then toss with cooked pasta.

12 **Surprise Packages:** Arrange salmon fillets on squares of lightly greased foil. Top with sliced bell peppers and sliced leeks, sprinkle with white wine, season with salt and pepper, and fold the foil into a packet, leaving some air space. Place the packets on a baking sheet and cook for 10 to 12 minutes at 375°F. Serve with lemon wedges.

GIVE IT A TRY

Roasted peppers, sold in jars, are delicious additions to appetizer trays, sandwiches, and whole grain dishes. To make your own, arrange whole bell peppers on a baking sheet and roast at 400°F for about 45 minutes, rotating every 15 minutes, until the skins are evenly blackened. Cool, slice into strips, and scrape off the skins with a sharp knife.

12 WAYS TO USE Potatoes

Potatoes are America's most popular vegetable. They are also nutrient-dense and a staple food in cuisines around the world. One medium potato, with skin, has more potassium than a banana, provides almost half the daily value of vitamin C, is a good source of vitamin B6, and contains no fat, sodium, or cholesterol. Amid the hundreds of different types of potatoes, popular varieties include russets, reds, fingerlings, blues, purples, yellows, and whites — each offering different textures and tastes. Experiment in your kitchen to find ways to make potatoes central to quick and easy meals.

QUICK FACTS

1 medium potato

Calories:	147
Fat:	0.2g
Sodium:	34mg
Carbs:	33g
Fiber:	5g
Protein:	3.6g

BREAKFAST

1. **One-Pan Meal:** Peel and shred several potatoes, sauté in a bit of olive oil until lightly browned, and top with any or all of the following: a beaten egg, black beans, diced tomatoes, grated cheese. Toss and cook until all ingredients are hot.

2. **With Eggs:** Reheat cooked, sliced potatoes and tuck into an omelet or serve as a side with scrambled eggs.

APPETIZERS & SNACKS

3. To make skordalia, a dip that can be used like hummus, mash several cooked potatoes with diced garlic, almonds, olive oil, lemon juice, and vinegar, and season with salt and pepper.

SALADS

4. Cook potatoes according to your favorite method. While still warm, cut into chunks and toss with a dressing made from vinegar, olive oil, a little Dijon mustard, and your choice of chopped, fresh herbs. Serve warm or cold.

SOUPS & STEWS

5. **Winter Favorite:** Sauté a chopped onion, 3 chopped leeks (white and light green parts only), and a few cloves of garlic in olive oil. Add about 1 pound peeled, chopped potatoes and 4 cups vegetable or chicken stock. Cook for about 20 minutes, partially covered, until the potatoes are very soft. Season with salt and pepper to taste.

6 **Thickener:** Add a peeled, diced potato, cook for 15 minutes, mash the potato against the side of the pan, and let it "melt" into the liquid to thicken soups and stews.

EASY COOKING

7 **Ultimate Comfort Food:** Boil and mash or bake a potato at 400°F until soft, and enjoy with olive oil, salt and pepper, a spoonful of guacamole or salsa, or chopped fresh tomatoes and herbs.

8 **Oven Fries:** Cut unpeeled potatoes into wedges, toss lightly with olive oil, and roast on a baking sheet at 400°F for about 20 minutes, turning once, until lightly browned.

9 **Microwave Tip:** Make a "baked" potato in a microwave by cutting a wedge (⅛-inch wide and ½-inch deep) out of each potato, to let the steam escape. Place in a microwave-safe dish, and microwave on high, uncovered, for 10 to 12 minutes, until soft. Use oven mitts to remove the dish.

10 **Simple Dinner:** Cut unpeeled potatoes into thick wedges, toss with olive oil, cumin, smoked paprika, and salt, and roast on a baking sheet at 425°F for 25 minutes, or until crisp. Top with cheese, black beans, and/or sliced olives, and bake for 5 minutes longer.

ON THE GRILL

11 **Potluck Favorite:** Spray a 9 x 9 x 2-inch foil pan liberally with nonstick cooking spray, build layers of thinly sliced onion, potato, and cheese, cover tightly with foil, and grill the pan over medium heat for about 1 hour.

12 Precook potatoes by baking, boiling, or microwaving until just barely tender. Cut into chunks, thread onto skewers with vegetables and your choice of seafood, chicken, or meat. Grill over medium-high heat for about 10 minutes, brushing with a little olive oil during the last few minutes of cooking.

TIME-SAVING TIP

Combine leftover mashed potatoes with a sautéed onion and vegetable broth for an instant soup.

12 WAYS TO USE Squash (Winter)

QUICK FACTS

1 cup cubed butternut squash	
Calories:	63
Fat:	0.14g
Sodium:	6mg
Carbs:	16g
Fiber:	2.8g
Protein:	1.4g

Winter squashes grow in a variety of sizes, shapes, colors, and flavors that share similar textures, making them mostly interchangeable in recipes. Dark green acorn, buttercup, and colorful delicata squashes are the smallest; cream-colored butternut, shaped like an elongated pear, is one of the most popular; and banana, turban, and hubbard squashes are among the largest. All need to ripen on the vine, which is why they appear at farmers markets toward the end of the season. If cutting, seeding, peeling, and chopping a hard-skinned winter squash seems daunting, shop for cubed squash, with all the prep work done for you. Winter squash provides plenty of nutritional benefits, including vitamins A and C, potassium, and carotenoid antioxidents. It's also wonderfully versatile, holding up well to baking, braising, mashing, puréeing, roasting, simmering, sautéing, steaming, and stir-frying.

BREAKFAST

1. Combine cubed squash with cooked, cubed potatoes when making home fries.

APPETIZERS & SNACKS

2. Save seeds from a large squash, clean on paper towels, put in a bowl and toss with a little olive oil and salt. Arrange in a single layer on a baking sheet lined with parchment paper and bake at 200°F for about 20 minutes, until lightly browned. Let cool before serving.

SALADS

3. **Slaw:** Grate peeled squash chunks in a food processor or with a box grater, combine with grated carrots, chopped red bell pepper, and sliced scallions, and toss with peanut vinaigrette.

4. **Picnic Perfect:** Combine cooked, diced squash with cooked quinoa, chopped, dried cranberries, and chopped, toasted pecans. Sprinkle with a spoonful of maple syrup.

SOUPS & STEWS

5   **Tasty Addition:** Add peeled, diced squash to lentil soups, vegetable soups, and chili for the last 20 minutes of cooking time.

6   **Fall Favorite:** Sauté diced, peeled squash with 2 diced, peeled apples, and a diced onion. Sprinkle with cumin and cinnamon, cook for a few minutes, add some apple cider, stir, and add vegetable stock. Cover and simmer for about 30 minutes. Purée and serve garnished with peanuts.

EASY COOKING

7   **Roasted:** Cut the peeled squash into 1-inch chunks, toss with olive oil, and roast at 400°F for about 30 minutes.

8   **Steamed:** Cut the peeled squash into 1-inch chunks, and steam for about 10 minutes or until tender.

9   **Mashed:** Bake and mash peeled squash chunks, add a bit of olive oil, and season with salt and pepper. For a special treat fold in a few peeled, chopped clementines or oranges and sprinkle with cinnamon.

10   **Secret Ingredient:** Build a layer or two of grated squash in your next lasagna.

11   **Grain Partner:** Add peeled, cooked, cubed squash to cooked barley, farro, or other whole grains. Serve sprinkled with lemon juice and diced fresh herbs.

12   **Boats:** Cut acorn or delicata squash in halves, scoop out the seeds and any stringy parts, brush with olive oil, arrange in a baking dish, add water a depth of about ¼ inch, and bake at 400°F for about 25 minutes. Remove from the oven, fill each half with a mixture of brown rice, chopped scallions, and currants, top with grated cheese and bake for 10 minutes longer, or until the squash is tender.

TIME-SAVING TIP

Place peeled, chopped squash in a microwave-safe dish, add a spoonful of water, cover, and microwave for about 6 minutes.

12 WAYS TO USE Sweet Potatoes

QUICK FACTS

1 cup cubed
sweet potato

Calories:	114
Fat:	0.1g
Sodium:	73mg
Carbs:	27g
Fiber:	4g
Protein:	2.1g

Yes, sweet potatoes are pretty to look at when you cut them open, but that bright orange flesh is also a nutrition superstar, and a source of vitamin A and beta-carotene. (Eat with a healthy fat, such as olive oil, to get the full benefit.) You can also find purple and white varieties. Store them in a cool, dark place; don't refrigerate. They will discolor as they are exposed to air, so cook immediately after peeling and cutting. Grate directly into batters, or put them in a bowl with water to cover. Substitute cooked mashed sweet potatoes for canned pumpkin in holiday pies and breads, or mash and combine with mashed potatoes.

BREAKFAST

1. Sauté a peeled, diced sweet potato with some diced onion and a diced red pepper in an oven-proof skillet until tender. Add diced kale or spinach and cook for 1 to 2 minutes, until the greens are wilted. Cover with 6 eggs beaten with 1 cup milk and bake at 350°F for about 15 minutes, until set. Cut into wedges.

DRINKS

2. Combine a cooked sweet potato, a banana, plain Greek yogurt, and soy milk in a blender. Mix until smooth.

SALADS

3. Combine cooked quinoa, diced cooked sweet potatoes, chopped dried cranberries, and diced arugula, and toss with maple vinaigrette.

SOUPS & STEWS

4. **Weekday Dinner:** Sauté an onion and a peeled, chopped sweet potato in olive oil in a large pot for about 5 minutes. Add a can of drained, rinsed black beans, cumin, chili powder, salt, pepper, and 1 cup vegetable broth. Bring to boil, reduce the heat, and simmer for 20 minutes, or until the sweet potato is soft. Serve with any cooked whole grain.

5. **Winter Favorite:** Sauté an onion, 2 apples, and several peeled, diced sweet potatoes in olive oil in a large pot, for about 10 minutes. Add 1 cup cider, cumin,

cardamom, and ginger, bring to a boil, reduce the heat to low, and simmer for about 5 minutes. Add several cups vegetable stock and simmer, partially covered, for about 30 minutes. Purée and season with salt and pepper.

EASY COOKING

6 **Baked:** Arrange whole, unpeeled sweet potatoes in a baking pan, prick each several times with a fork, and bake at 400°F for about 40 minutes, or until soft. Let cool slightly, cut into halves, mash, season with salt and pepper, and top with toasted coconut and pomegranate seeds.

7 **Braised:** Peel sweet potatoes, cut into 1-inch slices, and arrange in a baking dish. Combine a little maple syrup with cider, pour over the slices, cover with foil, and bake at 350°F for about 40 minutes, until tender. Uncover and bake for 5 minutes longer, until lightly glazed. Sprinkle with chopped nuts.

8 **Microwave:** Prick a sweet potato in four or five places with a fork, and microwave for 5 to 8 minutes, until soft.

9 **Oven Fries:** Peel sweet potatoes, cut into wedges, put in a large bowl, and toss with olive oil, cumin, a bit of brown sugar, and salt. Arrange on a parchment paper-lined baking sheet and bake at 450°F for about 25 minutes, stirring once or twice. Switch the oven to broil and cook 5 minutes longer, until browned.

10 **Roasted:** Combine peeled, chopped sweet potatoes, chopped carrots, and chopped apples in a bowl, and toss with a bit of olive oil and orange juice. Transfer to a lightly greased baking sheet, and roast at 400°F for 30 minutes.

11 **Pasta Meal:** Sauté a diced sweet potato in olive oil until soft, sprinkle with balsamic vinegar, add a few handfuls of chopped greens, toss until wilted, and add to cooked pasta.

12 **Chopped Dinner:** Sauté peeled, diced sweet potato, diced red onion, diced zucchini, and diced bell peppers in a large frying pan until soft. Add any cooked whole grain, and heat through.

GIVE IT A TRY

At your next campfire, wrap sweet potatoes in heavy-duty aluminum foil and toss right into the coals to roast for about 1 hour. Remove, let cool slightly, cut in halves, and enjoy.

12 WAYS TO USE Tomatoes

America's second most popular vegetable (edged out by potatoes), tomatoes are rich in potassium and the carotenoids, lycopene, and beta-carotene that are associated with chronic disease prevention. Choices are dizzying, from delicate, striped, red, yellow, and green heirloom varieties to plum, cherry, and grape tomatoes in a rainbow of colors. For the best flavor seek out tomatoes grown locally, in season. Store at room temperature, unless they are overripe and you need to hold them for a day or two in the refrigerator. Tomatoes are perfect partners for many foods, and when perfectly ripe are delicious simply sliced and sprinkled with salt.

QUICK FACTS

1 medium tomato

Calories:	22
Fat:	0.2g
Sodium:	6mg
Carbs:	4.8g
Fiber:	1.5g
Protein:	1.1g

BREAKFAST

1 Sauté a sliced tomato in a little olive oil or broil it until soft and enjoy on toast.

APPETIZERS & SNACKS

2 **Bruschetta:** Slice a baguette, toast lightly, and rub the slices with a cut garlic clove. Coarsely grate one or two very ripe tomatoes and slather the resulting pulp on top of the toasted bread. Drizzle with olive oil and sprinkle with salt.

3 **Simple Tart:** Arrange sliced, fresh tomatoes on whole wheat tart dough or puff pastry. Sprinkle with chopped fresh herbs, crumbled or grated cheese, salt and pepper, and bake according to package directions.

4 **Salsa:** Chop fresh tomatoes, jalapenos, onion, and cilantro, and combine in a bowl with a squeeze of lime and a pinch of salt.

SALADS

5 **Caprese:** Slice tomatoes, drizzle with olive oil, sprinkle with salt and pepper, and interleave with slices of fresh mozzarella cheese and basil leaves.

6 **Panzanella:** Toss roughly chopped tomatoes, finely chopped red onion, diced olives, and a few rinsed, diced capers, olive oil, and balsamic vinegar in a large bowl; add chunks of day-old bread. Cover and let sit at room temperature for several hours to allow the bread to soak up the juices. Garnish with diced basil or parsley.

7   **Summer Favorite:** Combine halved cherry tomatoes with shaved shallots, fresh herbs, and feta cheese. Toss with vinaigrette and let sit at room temperature for about an hour.

8   **Delicious Lunch:** Hollow out a large, ripe tomato, leaving the bottom intact. Chop the tomato flesh and combine with canned tuna, roasted chicken, or cooked quinoa, herbs, celery, olive oil and vinegar. Stuff into the tomato.

DRESSINGS & SAUCES

9   Combine chopped, fresh tomatoes with basil, oregano, minced garlic, olive oil, salt and pepper, and cook over medium-low heat to make a thick sauce for pasta or chicken.

SANDWICHES, ETC.

10   Arrange halved plum tomatoes in a lightly oiled baking dish, sprinkle with salt and pepper, and bake at 250°F for several hours, until lightly browned. Cool and add to sandwiches and wraps.

SOUPS & STEWS

11   Combine fresh tomatoes with tomato juice, onions, bell peppers, salt, and pepper in a blender or food processor to make gazpacho. Blend to a chunky consistency and add a splash of red wine vinegar and a drizzle of olive oil. Serve chilled.

EASY COOKING

12   Cut 2 pints of cherry tomatoes in halves, sprinkle with salt, and drizzle with olive oil. Cover and let sit at room temperature for 4 to 6 hours, tossing occasionally. Cook your favorite type of pasta and toss with the juicy tomatoes.

GIVE IT A TRY

Slice green tomatoes, sprinkle with olive oil, season with salt and pepper, and bake at 400°F for about 15 minutes. Use in wraps and salsa.

12 WAYS TO USE Zucchini

Zucchini is famous for its overabundance in summer gardens, but don't let its common charm deter you from exploring the many ways to use this culinary staple. Zucchini adds its demure flavor and bulk to all kinds of dishes, from pastas to soups to baked goods. Slow cooking brings out its full squash flavor, but it also holds its own in stir-fries and quick sautés. Like other types of summer squash, zucchini has a thin skin and tender flesh, making it easy to prepare and quick to cook. If you add minced zucchini to warm cooked brown rice, farro, quinoa, or couscous, the heat of the grains will gently cook the zucchini. With a 1-cup serving offering a mere 20 calories and more than 30% of the recommended daily value of vitamin C, it makes a healthy addition to any meal.

BREAKFAST

1. Dice zucchini, wrap in paper towels, pat to remove some of the moisture, and add to a frittata, omelet, or quiche.

APPETIZERS & SNACKS

2. **Fancy Toast:** Brush baguette slices with olive oil and toast until golden, then top with ricotta, sautéed zucchini rounds, a squeeze of lemon juice, and salt and pepper.

3. **Raw:** Include sliced zucchini sticks on your next crudité platter.

SALADS

4. Mix finely diced zucchini into a chopped salad.

SANDWICHES, ETC.

5. Salt grated zucchini and let it drain in a colander for about 30 minutes. Pat dry on paper towels and sauté in olive oil until it mimics the consistency of caramelized onions. Use hot or cold in sandwiches and wraps.

SOUPS & STEWS

6 Add diced zucchini to vegetable soups and chili.

EASY COOKING

7 **Sautéed:** Slice zucchini into thin rounds and sauté in olive oil with garlic and onions over low heat for about 30 minutes. Serve as a side, mixed into pasta, or on top of couscous.

8 **Baked:** Slice a zucchini lengthwise and lay the halves on a baking sheet, cut-side up. Brush with olive oil and sprinkle with finely grated Parmigiano Reggiano and pepper. Bake at 400°F for 12 to 15 minutes, until the cheese is browned and the squash is tender.

9 **Steamed:** Steam ¼-inch-thick zucchini rounds on the stovetop. Drizzle with olive oil and season with chopped fresh chives or dill.

10 **Oven Fries:** Cut zucchini into strips, lightly salt, and place in a colander to drain for 30 minutes. Dip the strips into beaten egg, then breadcrumbs, and bake on a lightly greased baking sheet at 400°F for about 20 minutes, or until lightly browned.

11 **Pasta Substitute:** Make zucchini "noodles" using a mandolin, vegetable peeler, or spiralizer. Steam for about 2 minutes and top with your favorite sauce.

ON THE GRILL

12 Slice zucchini lengthwise into ¼-inch strips, brush with olive oil, season with salt and pepper, and grill. Enjoy the grilled slices on their own or in sandwiches.

TIME-SAVING TIP

Dice leftover cooked zucchini and add to tuna or chicken salad.

Whole Grains

Whole grains are a must in any vegetable lover's pantry, as few other foods can so beautifully transform a medley of produce into a hearty, satiating meal. The perfect partner to any vegetable, whole grains also lend a rich variety of flavors, textures, and aromas to your cooking.

To 1 cup of...	Add this much water or broth:	Bring to a boil, then simmer for:	Yields:
Amaranth	2 cups	20 to 25 minutes	3 ½ cups
Barley, hulled	3 cups	45 to 60 minutes	3 ½ cups
Buckwheat	2 cups	20 minutes	4 cups
Bulgur	2 cups	10 to 12 minutes	3 cups
Cornmeal (polenta)	4 cups	25 to 30 minutes	2 ½ cups
Couscous, whole wheat	2 cups	10 minutes (heat off)	3 cups
Kamut® grain	4 cups	Soak overnight, then cook 45 to 60 minutes	3 cups
Millet, hulled	2 1/2 cups	25 to 35 minutes	4 cups
Oats, steel cut	4 cups	20 minutes	4 cups
Pasta, whole wheat	6 cups	8 to 12 minutes (varies by size)	Varies
Quinoa	2 cups	12 to 15 minutes	3+ cups
Rice, brown	2 1/2 cups	25 to 45 minutes (varies by variety)	3–4 cups
Rye berries	4 cups	Soak overnight, then cook 45 to 60 minutes	3 cups
Sorghum	4 cups	25 to 40 minutes	3 cups
Spelt berries	4 cups	Soak overnight, then cook 45 to 60 minutes	3 cups
Wheat berries	4 cups	Soak overnight, then cook 45 to 60 minutes	3 cups
Wild rice	3 cups	45 to 55 minutes	3 1/2 cups

Information provided by the Whole Grains Council

wholegrainscouncil.org